Clever Kid Guide to Superstitions

S.E. Harrison

DEEP STANCE MEDIA

Print Book ISBN 978-1-998568-00-0
E-Book ISBN 978-1-998568-01-7
Version 1.0

Book written and designed by S.E. Harrison
Illustrations generated by DALL-E, an AI program developed by OpenAI

Dedicated to those who
make their own luck.

Introduction

Welcome to the *Clever Kid Guide to Superstitions*—a journey into the curious and often quirky world of beliefs that have fascinated people for centuries! This book is packed with more than 100 superstitions from around the globe, each brought to life with a humorous illustration and a mention of where it all began.

Superstitions are those strange, funny, and sometimes spooky beliefs that tell us what to do (or not do) to avoid bad luck or attract good fortune. Whether it's tossing salt over your shoulder, avoiding black cats, or never opening an umbrella indoors, these traditions have been passed down through generations. But here's the fun part: while most superstitions aren't backed by science, they give us a fascinating glimpse into the history, culture, and imagination of people from all walks of life.

So why should you care about these old tales in today's modern world? First of all, learning about superstitions is *entertaining*! They often make us laugh, scratch our heads, or even jump a little when we hear them. Ever wondered why some people refuse to walk under a ladder or why breaking a mirror is said to bring seven years of bad luck? These strange rules make for some pretty amusing stories, and the illustrations in this book will help you see the humor in them.

But there's more to it than just having a good laugh. Understanding superstitions is also *educational*. Each superstition you'll find in this book comes from a different part of the world, offering a peek into the customs and traditions of various cultures.

Even though we know that many superstitions aren't scientifically proven, they still play a big role in human history. They show us how people used to explain the world around them, especially when they didn't have all the facts or technology we have today. By learning about these beliefs, we gain a better understanding of how people think and how different societies are connected by shared ideas, even if those ideas might seem a little silly now.

So, as you flip through the pages of this book, get ready to be entertained by the weird and wonderful world of superstitions. Who knows—you might even start to see some of them in your own life! But whether you believe in them or not, these superstitions are sure to make you smile, spark your curiosity, and give you a new appreciation for the oddball traditions that have shaped cultures across the globe.

Happy reading, and remember: whether or not you're superstitious, it's always fun to be clever about it!

A bat flying into your house brings bad luck.

Origin: China

Breaking a mirror brings seven years of bad luck.

Origin: Ancient Rome

It's bad luck to give a watch as a gift.

Origin: China

A black cat crossing your path is bad luck.

Origin: Ancient Egypt

Finding a four-leaf cover brings good luck.

Origin: Ireland

Walking under a ladder is bad luck.

Origin: Ancient Egypt

Knocking on wood to ward off bad luck.

Origin: Various cultures

Burning or burying nail clippings so they can't be used in black magic.

Origin: Various cultures

Throwing salt over your left
shoulder to ward off bad
luck.

Origin: Ancient Rome

Horseshoes bring good luck.

Origin: Greece

Opening an umbrella indoors is bad luck.

Origin: Ancient Egypt

A rabbit's foot brings good luck.

Origin: Europe

Spilling salt brings bad luck.

Origin: Ancient Rome

Crossing your fingers for luck.

Origin: Ancient Europe

Picking up a penny brings good luck.

Origin: United States

Itchy palms mean you will receive money.

Origin: Various cultures

Saying "Bless you" when someone sneezes.

Origin: Europe

A broken clock brings bad luck.

Origin: Various cultures

Wearing clothes inside out for good luck.

Origin: United States

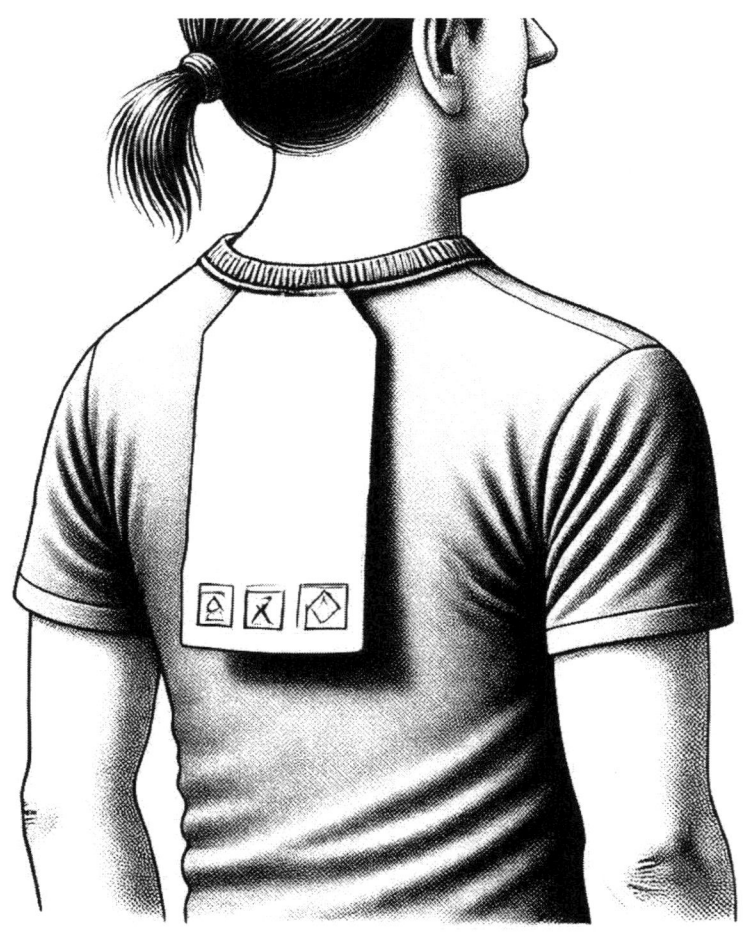

You can predict the future by counting crows.

Origin: England

Whistling at night will attract spirits or snakes.

Origin: South Korea

Seeing a shooting star brings good luck.

Origin: Various cultures

Carrying a lucky coin.

Origin: Various cultures

Hanging garlic to ward off evil spirits.

Origin: Europe

A cricket in the house brings good luck.

Origin: China

Bells ward off evil spirits.

Origin: Europe

Avoiding stepping on cracks in the sidewalk.

Origin: United States

Leaving a rocking chair rocking invites spirits.

Origin: Ireland

Blowing out birthday candles in one breath.

Origin: Germany

A ladybug landing on you brings good luck.

Origin: Europe

Making a wish on a wishbone.

Origin: Ancient Rome

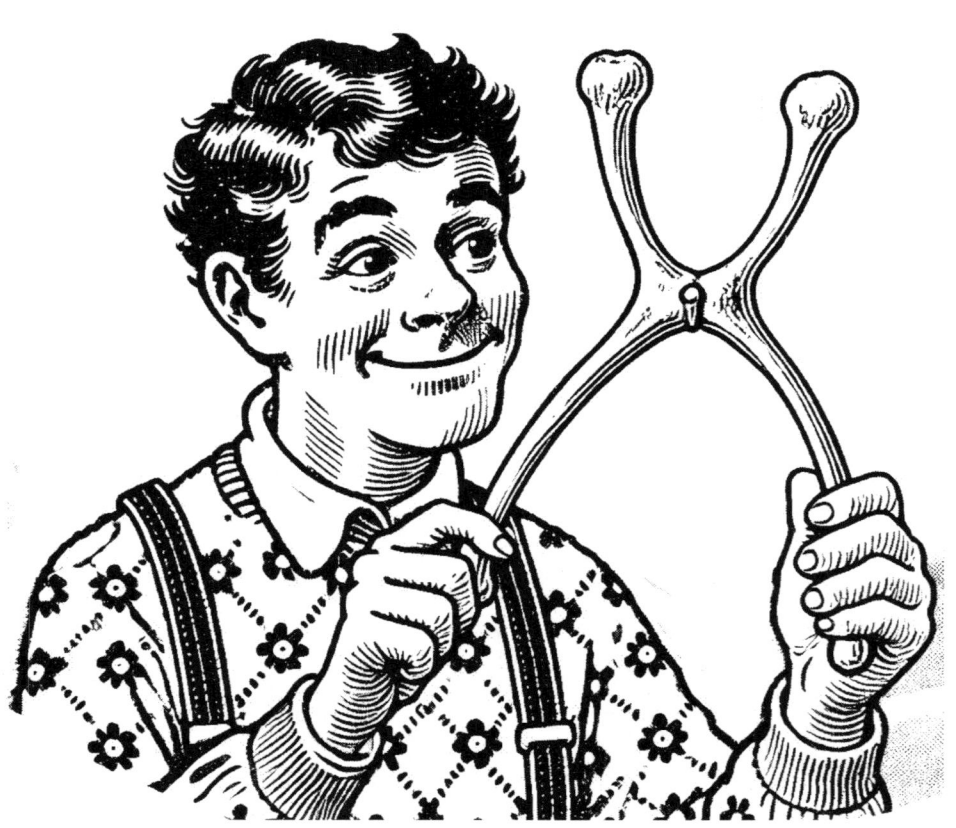

Carrying a charm or talisman.

Origin: Various cultures

Friday the 13th is bad luck.

Origin: Various cultures

Finding a spider in your home brings good luck.

Origin: England

A white cat crossing your path brings good luck.

Origin: United States

Spilling water behind someone going on a journey brings them good luck.

Origin: Serbia

Placing a mirror near the front door to deflect bad luck.

Origin: China

Swallowing gum takes seven years to digest.

Origin: United States

Breaking a glass brings good luck.

Origin: Jewish tradition

Sweeping dirt out the front door brings bad luck.

Origin: Various cultures

Saying "rabbit" or "white rabbit" on the first day of the month brings good luck.

Origin: England

A moth in the house brings a visitor.

Origin: Japan

Hanging a dreamcatcher to ward off bad dreams.

Origin: Native American

Walking backwards brings bad luck.

Origin: Various cultures

Whistling indoors invites bad luck.

Origin: Russia

Keeping a jar of salt in the kitchen for good luck.

Origin: Various cultures

Dropping a knife means a visitor is coming.

Origin: Various cultures

A ringing in the ears means someone is talking about you.

Origin: Various cultures

Finding a feather brings good luck.

Origin: Various cultures

A hiccup means someone is thinking of you.

Origin: Philippines

Meeting a black and white cat brings good luck.

Origin: England

Wishing upon a star.

Origin: Various cultures

Carrying an acorn for longevity.

Origin: England

Placing bread upside down brings misfortune.

Origin: France

A spider spinning a web means good luck.

Origin: Various cultures

Putting shoes on the table is bad luck.

Origin: Various cultures

Finding a pencil on the floor means good luck.

Origin: United States

A ringing phone when you think of someone means they are calling you.

Origin: Various cultures

Dreaming of a wedding means bad luck.

Origin: Various cultures

Seeing a beetle brings good luck.

Origin: Egypt

A single crow cawing brings bad luck.

Origin: Various cultures

Dropping scissors brings bad luck.

Origin: Various cultures

Carrying a piece of coal for good luck.

Origin: Scotland

Spilling wine during a toast brings good luck.

Origin: Greece

Stepping in dog poop brings good luck.

Origin: France

Seeing an owl during the day brings bad luck.

Origin: Egypt

A cat washing its face means visitors are coming.

Origin: Japan

Finding a pin brings good luck.

Origin: Various cultures

Putting your purse on the floor brings bad luck.

Origin: Various cultures

Saying "red sky at night, sailor's delight."

Origin: England

A picture falling off the wall means bad luck.

Origin: Various cultures

Hanging a horseshoe with ends up brings good luck.

Origin: Various cultures

Spilling pepper brings bad luck.

Origin: Various cultures

The number 4 is unlucky.

Origin: China

The number 7 is lucky.

Origin: Various cultures

Putting a hat on a bed brings bad luck.

Origin: United States

A bird flying into your window means bad luck.

Origin: Various cultures

Seeing a double rainbow brings good luck.

Origin: Various cultures

A bee flying into your house means visitors are coming.

Origin: Ireland

A dog howling at night brings bad luck.

Origin: Various cultures

A spider in the morning brings bad luck.

Origin: Various cultures

A bird chirping at your window means good luck.

Origin: Various cultures

Carrying a piece of silver for good luck.

Origin: Various cultures

Finding a button means good luck.

Origin: Various cultures

A black moth in the house means death.

Origin: Mexico

Spilling rice brings bad luck.

Origin: Various cultures

A bird pooping on your car brings good luck.

Origin: Russia

A lizard in the house brings good luck.

Origin: India

Seeing a deer means good luck.

Origin: Japan

Eating grapes on New Year's Eve brings good luck.

Origin: Spain

An itchy nose means someone is coming to visit.

Origin: Ireland

Seeing a white butterfly brings good luck.

Origin: England

Dropping a fork means a woman will visit.

Origin: Various cultures

Dropping a spoon means a man will visit.

Origin: Various cultures

A frog in the house brings good luck.

Origin: Japan

A person can harm you by giving you an "evil eye" (looking at you with envy or ill will).

Origin: Greece and Turkey

If someone sweeps over your feet with a broom, you'll never get married.

Origin: Brazil

A snake in the house brings good luck.

Origin: India

Seeing a red cardinal brings good luck.

Origin: United States

Cutting your hair during a new moon will make it grow thicker and faster.

Origin: India

Sleeping with your feet facing the door is bad luck.

Origin: China

Scanning this QR code to leave a review on Amazon will bring you good luck:

Also from
Deep Stance Media

www.deepstancemedia.com

Manufactured by Amazon.ca
Bolton, ON

40489133R00061